CEASEFIRE

Finding Peace When All You See Is Conflict

Chip Nightingale

Renown Publishing
www.renownpublishing.com

Ceasefire / Chip Nightingale
ISBN-13: 978-0-578-32836-2

Ceasefire by Chip Nightingale is a rich source of practical, biblical guidance for resolving every type of conflict. As Chip shares his own story, the reader soon realizes that the truth in this book has been hammered out on the anvil of life. Here's my recommendation: buy two copies, one to keep and one to share with a friend. It's that good.

Dr. Ray Pritchard
President, Keep Believing Ministries

Matthew 18 is always so much better when it involves someone else, isn't it? Whether [the context is] marriage, church, friendship, or leadership, this book reminds us to forgive immediately and to not take the bait of offense. It shows how to live out both sides of Matthew 18 and how love is always part of the solution.

Jack Schrontenboer

I have followed Chip's life and ministry for many years and appreciate his transparency. *Ceasefire* is an extension of who he is, not just what he does. He has given very practical and biblical insights.

Mike Calhoun
Pastor of Ministry Training, The Summit Church,
Raleigh, North Carolina

In loving memory of my dad, who helped thousands of lives around the world work through conflict.

And to my beautiful wife, who encouraged me to write this book. I know that you had to walk through a lot of pain as I learned how to work through conflict as a husband, business owner, coach, and pastor. Thank you for standing by me through it all.

CONTENTS

Foreword by Pastor David Ashcraft

For years, my unofficial staff motto has been: "Let's not do anything stupid to mess up what God is doing here!" Unfortunately, this motto has been necessary because churches are notorious for doing stupid things to mess up what God is doing. It's my observation that those stupid things most often involve the mishandling of conflict.

Serving as a pastor for over forty years, I've watched churches around the country implode due to the lack of skills to manage conflict wisely. All too often, stories are told of churches being ravaged by conflict. From a distance, my heart broke as the historic Dallas, Texas, church I grew up in shrank from 2,500 attendees down to fewer than 100 attendees before choosing to close its doors after years of ignoring wise conflict resolution practices.

As LCBC Church (Lives Changed By Christ) grew from a group of 150 people led by a staff of one (me) to now close to 20,000 people led by a staff of over 250, my driving passion has been to introduce more and more people to Jesus. A close second has been my passion to protect our church from the poison of relational conflict.

Unfortunately, a bachelor's degree in Business Administration from Texas Tech University, a master's degree in Theology from Dallas Theological Seminary, and a Doctor of Ministry degree from Trinity Evangelical Divinity School did not properly prepare me for the relational conflicts I would face as a pastor. Little did I know that only a few of these conflicts would involve differing theological or biblical views. Instead, my experience has been that it's the mishandling of relational issues that most often destroys churches and messes up what God is doing in His church.

When I first met Chip Nightingale, Chip and I bonded quickly over our shared passion for introducing more and more people to Jesus. Over the years, I've also been impressed with Chip's ability to mix the theological lessons he learned in the classroom with the lessons he's learned while serving as a leader in his home, in the church, in business, and while coaching sports. Because he has been seasoned by life, Chip is uniquely qualified to guide us through God's plan for conflict resolution.

As *Ceasefire* points out, the Bible gives us practical tools to handle and manage conflict wisely. These tools are not hidden in Scripture, but rather given to us in very clear and simple terms. However, we often ignore these clear and simple truths of the Bible when we're mired in conflict. Using his own personal stories and life experiences, Chip takes us back to the Bible and maps out for us a simple path to conflict resolution.

To follow this path, I first need to put the needs of others over my own self-interest. I need to stay humble and hold a modest view of my own importance. On a practical level, God's path involves approaching the person I'm in conflict with before going to anyone else. As I make that approach, I need to ask God to guide me and empower me so that I will be impartial, sincere, and open to reason in my discussion.

Painfully, what I know about myself is that I am often tempted to choose a different path when faced with conflict. But as Chip so aptly states, the path of refusing to put things right only leads to anger, bitterness, and resentment—all of which further damage our relationships. *Ceasefire* boldly challenges us to get it right and to follow God's path for handling conflict well.

Ceasefire is for business leaders, church leaders, and individuals who want to enjoy the many benefits of putting to use simple and practical biblical tools for handling conflict God's way. Additionally, *Ceasefire* is written in a way that lends itself well to use as a sermon series or as content for small group discussions.

How great it would be if our churches were known more for our love for one another than for breaking up over mishandled conflict! As Chip Nightingale concludes, "The church that handles conflict well will continue to grow stronger and will become a bright light in the community."

David Ashcraft
Senior Pastor, LCBC Church (Lives Changed By Christ)

.

Foreword by Pastor Chad D. Nightingale

We live in a world full of individuals who want to stand out. Every basketball player wants to be Michael Jordan. Every designer wants to be Joanna Gaines. Every pastor wants to be invited to join the T4G conference speaking list. We want to have the new idea. We want to discover something everyone else has missed. We all want to do great things.

Coaches and builders are individuals who constantly remind us of the fundamentals. If athletes want to be great, then they need to know the fundamentals of a sport. If designers want to be great, then they need to know how to keep the structure standing. If speakers want to be among the best, then they must know how to frame a message to communicate truth in an applicable way.

Chip is a coach and a builder. He isn't presenting us with some new idea or grand theological principle. Chip deals in the fundamentals. He is reminding us to do the things we know we should be doing. He is reminding us to practice those things we will not be recognized for doing. These principles will not make us great because most of these things will take place in private conversations. They are the basics of living the Christian life that have been ignored because they are not flashy and they require humility. But if we, as followers of Jesus, practice these things, it will change our lives forever and bring glory to the name of our Savior. I know that everyone desires to be known, but isn't it enough for believers that Jesus will be known if we live the way He has instructed us to live?

I urge you to engage in this book. Use it devotionally. Use it in small groups. Use it as a reminder of the things we all must do if we are going to walk in right relationship with God and man.

Pastor Chad D. Nightingale
Pastor, Author, Biblical Counselor,
Biblical Counseling Instructor

The Real Problem

There's something inspiring about a freshly constructed house. The unmarred floors, the white walls, and the smooth countertops promise lots of family moments just begging to take place. You can almost see the wool-socked feet sliding into the kitchen for dinner and the finger paintings being tacked onto the fridge.

When I started a construction business with my best friend in the early 2000s, we could smell success like new paint on drywall. We wanted to create perfect homes for imperfect people with king-sized dreams. Our business began by offering framing services and grew to offering full contracting solutions, which included roofing, siding, and custom trim work.

By the spring of 2005, our company had grown to fifteen employees, and we had the hope of many amazing opportunities. In the early months of that year, we signed a contract to build three large homes in West Michigan, all of which were going to be showcased in the Annual Kalamazoo Parade of Homes. All of the homes were in the 7,000 to 9,000 square-foot range. When we completed the homes, we would have enough money to cover the funds we had laid out to start the business. We had a good relationship with the company who offered us the job and didn't ask for anything upfront.

At the same time, we had contracted with two other companies to build two smaller houses on other prime properties. One of those smaller companies was owned by a Christian. Our hope was to use the funds we got from assembling the smaller homes to survive while we worked to bring the three larger ones into reality.

What we didn't know was that the company financing the three larger homes was having cash-flow problems and beginning to drown. When we went to collect the money, we discovered that the doors had shut overnight, and they had filed for bankruptcy. This was a huge blow to my partner and me.

Our saving grace was that we could collect the money for the smaller homes to stay afloat while we figured the other mess out. However, when we went to recover those funds, the company run by a Christian withheld the money as well. We were in serious trouble. After using up our line of credit and working feverishly for months, we were in danger of losing everything.

As a pastor's son, I took my father's advice and spoke to a couple of ministers about the best way to approach the situation. They both advised that we go to court to try to get the money back, and I began the process of suing the company building the smaller property that had not paid us. I had a wife and family, and the housing market was beginning to crash. I had never felt so pressured.

Finally, one day, the Lord got a hold of me. "Chip," He said patiently, "you haven't been trusting Me to provide for your needs. You've been trying to do this all on your own. I didn't tell you to take your Christian brother to court. I told you to love your enemies as yourself."

The very next morning, I asked the Lord to forgive me for failing to trust Him. I went to my lawyer's office and told him that I was canceling the suit. He tried to talk me out of it because we were close to winning, but my heart was telling me a different story.

My next stop was the headquarters of the now-defunct company where the Christian brother I was suing worked. The owner and his lawyer nervously brought out their paperwork and explained again why they hadn't been able to pay. I stopped them soon after they started.

"That's not why I'm here," I said.

Both men looked up at me with slightly raised eyebrows.

"I am here to ask my forgiveness for suing you. The past three months have been some of the worst in my life. The first thing I should have done was come to you directly to reach a solution, but that's not what I did. I was desperate for money, and I haven't treated you the way a fellow Christian should. Matthew 18:15 makes it very clear that when you have a conflict, you should go to the person you have a problem with before involving anyone else. I went to my lawyer this morning, and you should soon be getting the paperwork canceling the suit. Will you forgive me?"

The owner exhaled. His mouth dangled open a little as he continued to stare at me. Then he whispered something to his lawyer.

After the attorney left the room, the owner leaned in. His voice was hoarse, and his face was suddenly younger. He asked, "What is God doing in your life right now?"

I smiled. "To tell you the truth, I don't know. But I'm going on a mission trip this fall, and I know God can't take me to the next level in my life with Him until I've cleared my heart of all sin."

He grinned back at me. "So, what is this trip, and where are you going?"

"We're going to build a kitchen for someone in France, but we are short on money."

"About that," he began, "I was going to pay you, but, well, I know I've explained it. I have never seen anyone do what you did today. I want to be a part of whatever God is going to do in your life on this trip and in the future. How much is the cost of the kitchen?"

To my surprise, he pulled out his checkbook and wrote me a check for the exact cost of the project. Then, believe it or not, he continued to donate money to my ministry for the next several years. It was more than we could ever have received from those three homes.

DEALING WITH CONFLICT

I believe that one of the biggest problems facing the world today is that we don't know how to deal with conflict. We struggle in our homes, our workplaces, and our social environments because we're either burying our feelings or letting them shoot out in angry sparks like bottle rockets after dark.

In the twenty-five years of my adult life, there have been times when I've handled conflict well, and there have been times when I've blown it. I've come to realize that my main source of trouble when it comes to conflicts is that I'm valuing my own self-interest above the needs of others. If we're really honest, I think many of us would admit that the real problem is that we always want to be right.

Often we avoid confronting people because we're afraid of tensions getting high and angry sentiments being expressed. Ultimately, fear wins, and the conflict remains a pot of boiling water simmering in our hearts.

What I love about the Bible is that it gives us practical tools that, when applied, would make our lives so much more agreeable, even if we weren't believers. In Matthew 18, Jesus talked to a group of guys who were trying to determine who was going to be the greatest in the kingdom of heaven. He reminded them that their problem was their focus on themselves rather than on a world lost in sin and sorrow.

If we were to apply Jesus' advice today, we wouldn't deal with offenses by ignoring them or by condemning the people responsible. We would forgive endlessly, just as Jesus graciously forgives us.

I'm looking forward to exploring this further as we journey together through our study of Christian approaches to conflict.

The Process

It was one of those Little League games—you know, the ones where no one can wait for the lemonade and chips at the end because nothing else about the situation is fun. My kids were in a tournament and were learning lots of lessons the hard way. We were down 18–1 when a little island began to peek out of our ocean of defeat: my son, Evan, had one of the best plays I've ever seen.

The catcher saw a player trying to steal third base, and Evan had his glove ready. The ball rolled right in like a log into a stream, and Evan tagged the player out.

The only problem: the umpire wasn't watching.

He was on the other side of the field, plotting out his dinner menu or scanning the sky for UFOs. We didn't know what was running through his baseball-capped mind, but we did know that he wasn't doing his job. Fortunately, the other umpire at home plate had his eye on the game. He made the right call, and we got back to playing. At least, that was our plan.

The other coach on our team, seething with anger and frustration over our devastating loss, began to rip into the umpire who wasn't paying attention. His voice was loud, his face was flushed, and his finger was wagging. I couldn't believe what a fool he was making of himself! It's not like we would have won the game even if the umpire had been paying attention. Besides, they had ultimately made the right call.

The absent-minded umpire was so rattled by the ordeal that he lost any semblance of confidence in his skills. For the rest of the game, he had his mind on anything but the plays. In fact, his eyes never left the bench of the coach who had just leveled him in front of parents, kids, and coaches until he felt about as tall as the grass that was whittling away at third base.

FRUSTRATION AND OUR SOULS

Frustration causes us to do irrational things. In fact, much of the time, we end up wishing right away that we could just roll up what we said and put it back in our mouths like a stick of bubblegum.

Imagine what would have happened if that coach had handled the situation the way a Christian brother should have. What if he had put his arm around the distracted umpire and given him a little pep talk? "Hey, you know, you should have been the one making that call. Maybe next time you should be on this side of the field so you are in a better position to see the play."

How much different do you think that young umpire

would have felt? How much more confidence would he have had as he continued determining the game?

We see this happening in the church all the time. Folks get frustrated by the most bizarre things. They don't like the sermon, the color of the carpet, or the way the usher sniffles. If we had God's wisdom, we wouldn't approach these points of contention with the selfish ambition, pride, and anger we normally do. Instead, we would submit ourselves to God.

> *What causes quarrels and what causes fights among you? Is it not this, that your passions are at war within you? You desire and do not have, so you murder. You covet and cannot obtain, so you fight and quarrel. You do not have, because you do not ask. You ask and do not receive, because you ask wrongly, to spend it on your passions.*
> **—James 4:1–3**

Our conflict comes because we're thinking about ourselves and driven by our passions. We're focused on what we want instead of on God. We're expressing our desires and frustrations rather than the love we should have for our fellow beings, who are made in God's image.

Is there another way to deal with conflict? Is it possible to let people know what's bothering us without spewing angry words, irritation, and bitterness like a fire hydrant on a hot summer day?

James 4:6 tells us that "God opposes the proud but gives grace to the humble." If, as the body of Christ, we can learn how to handle conflict within the church, we can also develop the skills to handle it within our marriages and workplaces. God is supremely gracious to those of us who handle conflict with humility.

What exactly is humility? Humility is the ability to hold a modest view of yourself and your own importance. This can be difficult for everyone, but the results are worth working for.

Imagine how different your marriage would be if you were to learn to deal with conflict lovingly and patiently. Think about what would happen if you didn't stew over how badly your spouse was hurting your pride. Instead, you could address the injury with gentleness and compassion, reminding yourself of your own shortcomings as a spouse and how you would like them to be handled if your spouse were speaking to you about them.

In the workplace, what would happen if we were to approach one another with honesty and kindness when we felt disrespected? What if we had a method of dealing with conflict that didn't involve gossiping, complaining, or getting our supervisors involved right away? What if we were sincerely looking for a positive resolution to our problem rather than a boost to our ego?

We would probably be a lot more productive, and our relationships would yield plenty of good fruit. Unfortunately, many of us grew up in homes where conflicts were either avoided or allowed to explode in raging words and actions. There's a better way, and it's spelled out in a handy little guidebook called the Bible.

THE MATTHEW 18 PRINCIPLE

As a pastor, I've had plenty of people come to me when they had an issue with someone else in the congregation. My response is always: "Have you spoken to this person?"

Sometimes folks ask me to go along for the confrontation. Again, my response is: "You need to go to this person alone first."

Twice at the beginning of my ministry, I went along with someone to approach another member of the congregation who had hurt them. I immediately regretted my decision. What I discovered was that there was a lot more involved in the dispute than I had originally been told, and I was in the middle of a conflict in which I didn't belong.

Parents know how this works. One of your kids is using a toy another one wants, and the one who wants the toy grabs it out of the other sibling's hand. The little cherub who was playing with the toy first will then hit or yell out of frustration. Before you know it, bitter words are flying, and you end up grounding everyone because the situation snowballs completely out of control.

Matthew 18:15–20 gives us quite a different take on handling conflict:

> *If your brother sins against you, go and tell him his fault, between you and him alone. If he listens to you, you have gained your brother. But if he does not listen, take one or two others along with you, that every charge may be established by the evidence of two or three witnesses. If he refuses to listen to them, tell it to the church. And if he*

refuses to listen even to the church, let him be to you as a Gentile and a tax collector. Truly, I say to you, whatever you bind on earth shall be bound in heaven, and whatever you loose on earth shall be loosed in heaven. Again I say to you, if two of you agree on earth about anything they ask, it will be done for them by my Father in heaven. For where two or three are gathered in my name, there am I among them.

Most of the time, when we have a problem with someone, we go to someone else first. We know that there will be a lot of strife if we go to the person with whom we're angry and vent our frustrations, so we look for someone else to listen and take our side. What ends up happening is that we create an even bigger problem than we started with.

Not one time does the Bible say that we should first go to another believer or the pastor, but we've created a culture in which our pastors want to be the point people for conflict. This role keeps them informed about the latest news in their congregations and fills them with pride as they become a kind of divine mediator.

In other churches, elders are assigned to oversee a group of people. If a conflict arises in the group, the elders are in charge of arbitrating it. Again, this is not a principle we find in Scripture.

The Bible tells us to go to our brother *first*.

Imagine what that would look like. Let's say that you're hurt by the way someone spoke to your child or you saw two church members laughing when you said something foolish. Your natural instinct may be to find a buddy and complain or even to find a new church.

Instead, you could go directly to the person who hurt your feelings and speak the truth in love. You may find that there are some things going on in that person's life you didn't even know about. Since no peer group or church is perfect, this could end up saving you a lot of loss, pain, and secrecy. You would be letting others know how you expect to be treated without acting prideful.

When my daughter, Emily, comes to me with a problem, I always want to take her side and defend her right away. Isn't that how we act when we're offended on behalf of our children? However, when we confront the situation in love, we usually find that there's a bigger picture. Someone might have had a bad day or be dealing with other issues in his or her home life. The behavior might not have been about us at all. We need to be open to hearing the other side of the story and willing to resolve the conflict in love. This will lead to a more peaceable understanding that will allow us to live together in harmony.

The principle of Matthew 18 is one we would be wise to heed. Don't involve anyone else until you first discuss your problem with your offender.

BASKETBALL AND MEEKNESS

I had been coaching girls' basketball for a little while when I realized that girls need a different type of conditioning than the fellas I was used to coaching. Boys love to get out on the court and follow one another's lead while they advance toward their goal. Girls, however, aren't comfortable just reacting to the moves of other players. Instead, they want to have lots of structure for their offensive and defensive strategies. They need a clear blueprint they can follow, and they want someone to walk them through the game plan beforehand.

I realized that I just wasn't good at creating the types of organized strategies the girls on my team needed, so I hired someone else to come onto our coaching team and teach the girls the basic fundamentals of offense.

Since I was still the head coach, he kept asking me, "Are you okay with me doing this?"

Finally, I had to tell him, "You don't understand. I hired you to help with the offensive work. I trust you. Just do your job."

We live in a culture in which those in charge love to be consulted. As a head coach, I know that I'm going to be blamed if things fall apart. As a lead pastor, I know that I'm going to be held responsible if people leave the church because they aren't happy. This is true whether I like it or not and whether or not I had anything to do with what happened. There's a tendency to say, "Well, I'm going to be held accountable, so just do what I say." However, I reached a point where I had to admit that there are some things I'm not good at, and I left authority in those areas to someone else.

James 3:13 asks us, "Who is wise and understanding among you? By his good conduct let him show his works in the meekness of wisdom." When we approach someone, we need to do so with a spirit of humility.

In verses 16 and 17 of James 3, he goes on to tell us, "For where jealousy and selfish ambition exist, there will be disorder and every vile practice. But the wisdom from above is first pure, then peaceable, gentle, open to reason, full of mercy and good fruits, impartial and sincere."

Many times when we approach people, we go to them because we're mad. We're frustrated, and we don't want to feel pain anymore. We want them to fall in line, convinced that would rid us of our unbearable vexation. But unloading our feelings does nothing to help the situation. If we're jealous, we may even go so far as to create false or exaggerated accusations.

Verse 16 warns us that when we approach someone with jealousy or selfish ambition, disorder will result. Everyone will become angry, and we will continue to get more boiled up as charges are made against us in return. We want to defend and protect ourselves, and so will the person with whom we're arguing.

But with a little wisdom, it's possible to have a productive conversation. We need to take a step back and look at the whole picture. What other things might that person have been feeling, and what could have driven him or her to cause us pain? Have we ever felt or acted in a similar way?

Often a great way to approach people who have offended us is to ask them what's going on with them. Are there any frustrations or struggles at home or with their kids? Are they having trouble providing for their families? Understanding the situation completely will make us a lot more compassionate. We can approach the situation in a way that is impartial, sincere, and open to reason.

QUITTING CHURCH

In 2018, an article appeared in Fox News about why people are quitting church. The author, Chris Sonksen, highlighted how Americans are beginning to "treat church like a product to consume."[1]

Think about it. Have you ever become irritated when you didn't like the worship set or if the church cafe didn't have your favorite coffee? Churches today try to make the worship experience pleasant for believers, but this can lead to some dangerous complacency and selfishness on the part of the congregation.

Sonksen went on to state:[2]

> When we treat church like a product, we consume until our needs are no longer met. When we treat church like a family, we fundamentally understand there are no perfect churches. Like family, every church comes with broken people. That includes the church leadership.
>
> ...Frustration is never content until it's expressed. If we have frustrations that we have not dealt with, those same frustrations will most likely follow us to the next church.
>
> ...When we leave because we don't get our way, it will set a poor example for others.

Your concerns may be valid, and your hurt feelings may be justified. Your feelings are, at least, yours to feel. The problem comes in how you deal with them. If you're offended by someone, especially someone in church leadership, there's a tendency to abandon your church completely, but what you will find in the next church is more broken people with the potential to hurt you.

Sonksen asks Christians to do some thinking before we choose to leave a church:

> Before we leave, have we done everything we can to make peace in the situation? ... Without attacking, have we expressed our concerns with the church leadership? Are we willing to get our hands dirty and become a part of the solution? Have we prayed about leaving? These are tough questions that force us to get real.
>
> Before we quit church, we need to make sure we take the separation seriously.

The Matthew 18 principle is critical here. When you're dealing with an offense, you need to speak to your offender one-on-one before getting anyone else involved. It's only when your brother won't hear you that you bring one or two others along with you. This is so there will be witnesses to your attempt to resolve the situation peacefully. Only then should you involve the church. Finally, you should allow your brother to live in sin until he realizes his offense. If you are humble and peace-loving in your attitude, the conflicts will rarely get past the first step.

What would happen if we really were pure, impartial, and open to reason as James tells us to be? Chances are that we could reconcile and not immediately lose our church family. Resolving conflict in a biblical manner can result in a church body that is even stronger. If our Christian brothers and sisters can turn around and begin resolving family and workplace conflicts with the same attitude and approach, others will take notice, respect Christians more, and maybe even turn toward God.

We trust our heavenly Father because He loves us unconditionally. When we show our brothers and sisters unconditional love, they will respond by trusting us, even during times of conflict. Sometimes we may have to agree to disagree. If we are going to remain a strong body, we need to trust each other even when we don't see eye to eye. Unfortunately, our modern church has a history of handling conflict poorly.

The next time you have a disagreement with someone, take a leap of faith and resolve the conflict using the biblical process outlined in Matthew 18. Talk to the person one-on-one, allowing your humility and willingness to see the other person's side to take center stage. The result may be a church family that sticks together no matter what. Like any healthy family, you can argue, make up, and get back to enjoying your fantastic meal.

Chapter One Questions

Question: What frustrations do you have that keep you from engaging with other people in a Christlike manner? How do these frustrations impact your relationship with others? How do they impact your relationship with God?

_____

_____

_____

_____

_____

_____

_____

_____

_____

_____

_____

Question: What is your initial response when someone hurts your feelings or you feel that someone has wronged you? Why do you think it's uncomfortable to go straight to the person with whom you have an issue? Have you ever approached a conflict by going straight to the person first? What was the result of that approach?

_____

_____

_____

_____

_____

_____

_____

_____

_____

_____

Action: Is there someone in your life who has offended you? Is there someone with whom you have a conflict or disagreement? How have you handled the situation thus far? Moving forward, review the process for addressing conflict outlined in Matthew 18 and apply it to the situation. Remember to approach the person with openness and love and to consider the bigger picture.

Chapter One Notes

_____

_____

_____

_____

_____

_____

_____

_____

_____

_____

_____

_____

_____

_____

_____

_____

_____

_____

Identifying Sin

Confronting those who have wronged you can be like a cold drink of water for a sunbaked soul. When you express your hurt responsibly, the burden of your hurt is lifted. Meanwhile, your offenders will learn and grow as long as they can own their part in the conflict. On the other hand, you also need to be willing to recognize and admit anything you have done that contributed to the conflict.

Refusing to do your part to make things right can put you on the path of sin. Staying bitter can make you prone to becoming angry, which can damage your current relationships. You may find that it's difficult to overlook offenses from your spouse or friend, so the chasm between you widens.

Anger, resentment, and pain can chip away at your spirit and cause mental and even physical problems. Bitterness can cause depression, which negatively affects the way you feel. You may experience anxiety, guilt, or feelings of worthlessness.

Your focus on the past may prevent you from enjoying current experiences. If you find that you can't savor the glow of a warm day or a belly laugh with your family, take a look at your past. Are there hurtful words or actions you still haven't forgiven?

Failure to forgive can also affect your sleeping and eating patterns. If your unsettled feelings are always driving you to the fridge for an extra scoop of ice cream, it may be time to examine your soul. Bitterness can even go so far as to affect your metabolism and immune system. You may be more likely to become sick or even live a shorter life if you have unresolved pain.[3]

The time you take to resolve a conflict in love is never wasted. In fact, the well-being of your body, soul, and spirit could depend on your being able to confront those who offend you with maturity.

How do you know when it's time for a Matthew 18-style confrontation? Is it when you don't like the way your Bible study leader chomps her gum? How about when you're offended by the jaunty style of the worship pastor with the Hawaiian shirt? Should you say something when you hear someone making fun of you? What about when you find out that your married friend is developing a romantic interest in his co-worker?

Matthew 18:15 is clear in stating that you are to confront your Christian brothers and sisters when they sin against you. It's important to understand that your being offended doesn't always mean that your brother or sister has sinned.

What kinds of offenses warrant a biblical confrontation? Let's take a look.

THE ORIGINS OF SIN

God is sovereign over all things, but He is *not* the author of sin. He "is light, and in him is no darkness at all" (1 John 1:5). In fact, God hates sin. Proverbs 8:13 reminds us that the "fear of the LORD is hatred of evil. Pride and arrogance and the way of evil and perverted speech I hate." If we love God, then we, too, will hate evil. Qualities such as arrogance and disregard for God's law will be off-putting to those of us with righteous hearts, and they are even more distasteful to God.

The origins of sin are in Satan, who was acting out of his own evil desire. He was tempted by his flesh and chose himself over God. When we sin, it's usually because we desire something for ourselves rather than for God.

Isaiah 14:12–14 describes a vision regarding Satan that was given to a king:

How you are fallen from heaven, O Day Star, son of Dawn! How you are cut down to the ground, you who laid the nations low! You said in your heart, "I will ascend to heaven; above the stars of God I will set my throne on high; I will sit on the mount of assembly in the far reaches of the north; I will ascend above the heights of the clouds; I will make myself like the Most High."

Satan was God's right-hand man, but he wanted more. He wanted to be like God. While we might never have told ourselves that we want to be God, many of us know what it's like to want more dominance. We may not get along with our boss or someone in authority over us, but if we're honest, we'll admit that it's not because the person is really all that bad. It's because we want to be the ones with that power. When we want something that's outside the realm of God's will for us, we're tempted. When we act on that desire, we sin.

Satan was thinking about sinning before he tried to rise above God. Why would God allow Satan to have the will to choose evil, knowing the catastrophe that would result? The answer is simple: God wants us to choose Him. He didn't make robots who would obey Him because they had no other possibility. There's no love in that.

How many of us run our homes as though our children should be little automatons who always obey us? Some of our insistence on obedience is for their protection, but other times we're just trying to create little yes-men and yes-women. We don't always take into account that every child is different. We should be tweaking our parenting style based on each child's God-given needs and strengths. Like God, we can love, provide reasonable limits, and still allow children to have their own will.

We can cater our style to be gentler with sensitive children and more honest with those who tend to be proud. If a child is autistic, we can introduce him or her to inspiring Christian music. A child who likes to build things might enjoy service projects, such as helping to make affordable dwellings for those less fortunate. Regardless, the decision to follow Christ ultimately lies with each individual person. Children who turn to faith without being coerced can become powerful witnesses to their world, both now and in the future.

SIN AND CHOICE

We actually have no idea how long Adam and Eve were in the Garden of Eden before they fell. When we first read Genesis, it can seem like a couple of days, but time had no value then. Adam and Eve weren't going to die, so there was no reason to measure time.

Satan was roaming around the Garden as one of God's angels before he disobeyed.

> *You were in Eden, the garden of God; every precious stone was your covering, sardius, topaz, and diamond, beryl, onyx, and jasper, sapphire, emerald, and carbuncle; and crafted in gold were your settings and your engravings. On the day that you were created they were prepared. You were an anointed guardian cherub. I placed you; you were on the holy mountain of God; in the midst of the stones of fire you walked. You were blameless in your ways from the day you were created, till unrighteousness was found in you. In the abundance of your trade you were filled with violence in your midst, and you sinned; so I cast you as a profane thing from the mountain of God, and I destroyed you, O guardian cherub, from the midst of the stones of fire.*
> *—Ezekiel 28:13–16*

Satan was covered in the kind of stuff you and I only see through windows at the mall. He had everything a created being could have dreamed of, but he wanted more. In the end, he chose himself over God. The author of sin was not Adam or Eve; it was Satan.

God's angel desired something that was not of God. The Lord didn't tempt him; his own nature did. He desired power, and it made him wicked.

When we are tempted, it's because we want something that's not in God's plan for us. It's not God who is tempting us. We know from reading Job that God can allow Satan to tempt us, but God doesn't create the temptations that beset us. Our Father believes in us and our love for Him, and He knows that we will fight for Him.

James 1:13–15 tells us that when we are tempted, we have no one to blame but ourselves:

> Let no one say when he is tempted, "I am being tempted by God," for God cannot be tempted with evil, and he himself tempts no one. But each person is tempted when he is lured and enticed by his own desire. Then desire when it has conceived gives birth to sin, and sin when it is fully grown brings forth death.

No one twists our arms and makes us do things we know aren't right. Sin happens when, because of our own selfishness, we act for our own benefit at the expense of others. Sin runs deep within us. Adam and Eve ate the fruit because they wanted to be more like God (Genesis 2:4–6).

Their flesh told them that they could have something more even though God had already told them, "I have given you everything you need." They let their sinful desires win out over their love for God.

The Greek word for sin is *hamartia*.[4] This is, literally, "a power exercising dominion over men." The hamartia in ancient literature is a fatal flaw that ultimately leads to the downfall of a hero. The Hebrew word for sin is *ḥāṭā'*, which means to fail or miss the goal.[5] This happens when we're looking for something besides God to become the answer to our human condition. When we sin, we are surrendering to a power that will, without a doubt, undo us.

When Jesus spoke about the confrontation of sin in Matthew 18, He wasn't suggesting that we have a serious conversation with someone who doesn't share our opinion. If we don't like the way someone raises his hands in worship or we don't agree with someone's parenting style, we aren't called to have a weighty talk. We should only approach someone in love when we know that sin has taken place.

That said, if we don't go to our brother or sister who has sinned, we ourselves are sinning because we have a command from God to open each other's eyes. Not calling out someone who has sinned means that we are failing to show Christ's love. Friction will remain that doesn't honor God.

How can we be certain that sin has occurred? What constitutes trying to put ourselves in God's place? Once again, let's break open the Bible.

THE TEN COMMANDMENTS

Sin was a real problem in the lives of the Jews before the law. They didn't know when they were sinning and when they weren't, because nothing was clearly defined. Then the Ten Commandments were wheeled onto the stage.

We find the first commandment in Exodus 20:3. God tells us to have no other gods before Him. Most of us could be confronted on this one. If we're honest, we know that there are a lot of things we prioritize above God.

The next three commandments tell us not to make idols, not to take the Lord's name in vain, and to keep the Sabbath day holy. Finally, we are told to honor our parents (Exodus 20:4–12). All of the first five commandments are telling us ways we can fail to love God.

The next five commandments, by contrast, let us know how we can fail to love people (Exodus 20:13–17). We are not to murder, commit adultery, or steal. We should not lie about our neighbor or covet what he has. When we fail to love people, we are failing to love God at the same time.

If you're honest, are there things here you need to work on? Many of us haven't committed murder or slipped into our neighbor's house to pilfer some jewelry. But how often do we wish that we had someone else's life when we look at social media? And how prone are we to put other things before God, such as family or work?

We know that there are seeds of sin in our hearts. If another Christian comes to you because he or she sees evidence of commandment-breaking in your life, you had better be listening. If you're the one doing the approaching, you have a responsibility as well. First Corinthians 13:4–7 tells us, "Love is patient and kind; love does not envy or boast; it is not arrogant or rude. It does not insist on its own way; it is not irritable or resentful; it does not rejoice at wrongdoing, but rejoices with the truth. Love bears all things, believes all things, hopes all things, endures all things."

When we approach someone in love, we are patient and kind. We aren't eager to point out the other person's flaws or boast about our own righteousness. We express our concern while conveying our love and respect for our Christian brother or sister. We let the person know how excited we are about the work God is doing in his or her life and how much we believe in him or her. A change in this person's heart would make him or her even more of a blessing to our heavenly Father.

POLITICAL PICNICS

One week, our church was having one of our famous picnics at a local park. Between our bites of burgers and frisbee tosses, we were surprised by a visit from a local political activist. He was going to share his agenda with us, whether we asked for it or not.

Fortunately, the folks in my church responded in a loving, mature way, and he ended up staying to hear a gospel message. I don't know whether or not he accepted it, but I do know that he was given a once-in-a-lifetime opportunity. If I had acted according to my flesh, that wouldn't have happened.

You see, I already knew about this man's political agenda. Several months before the picnic, we had been running against each other for a school board position. He had done everything in his power to make me look like an idiot, and I could have returned the favor during our holy barbeque.

By the grace of God, that's not what happened. Instead, I put my arm around him and said, "Listen, I'm so glad that you could be here today, and I'm proud of your desire to make a difference in our community. I have to tell you that I'm praying for the Lord's will to be done in your life."

Love, not our personal opinions, is what will help to change a person's heart. My personal preferences when it comes to our government may not align with those of everyone who walks into my church. My job is not to change their minds. Instead, I am supposed to love them and welcome them into a place where they can hear the truth about God and the Son who loves them.

It would actually have been wrong for me to call out sin in that man's life because he wasn't a believer. My responsibility was simply to love him the way Christ loved me before I followed Him.

Sin was never found in Jesus because He always chose God's plan over His own, even when He was being tempted. When we do the same, the blessings of our Father await us.

True Rest

Have you ever taken a break from your cell phone? How long did it last? Did you ever find yourself reaching into your pocket or purse out of habit, anxiety, or even hope?

When my wife and I visited Word of Life, we had to give up our electronics for two weeks. It was strange at first, and I was always wondering who could be trying to get a hold of me. Yet by the end of the trip, I had really begun to enjoy myself. My wife and I relaxed, did some camping, and slept a lot.

How many of us feel like we need a vacation after we come home from a trip? We don't feel rested because we just got busier, and we come back feeling even more tired. The truth is that we can't truly rest on vacation if there is no God on that vacation.

One of the things I find myself doing to avoid temptation is staying busy. I'll create repair projects for myself while I'm at church, and I'll play basketball when I get home. I find myself ignoring my family because I'm afraid that quiet time will come when we are all on our phones and tablets, and that's when I get tempted.

What I really need is to be filling myself up with more of God when I'm not in a hurry. If my flesh can't handle temptation, I need the people of God to surround me, pray for me, and lift me up. Additional items on my to-do list may provide a temporary distraction, but there will be no long-term change. I'm not going to find refreshment, peace, and encouragement in the things of this world. That kind of rest can come only from God.

When we're tempted, where do we go? Sin was found in Lucifer because of a choice he made to seek something other than God's plan. You don't have to do the same thing. No matter where you are in your life right now and what kind of work you're doing, you can be confident that God has you right where He wants you. There's something important that He wants to accomplish through you. If you lean into His plan, you'll be surprised at what He can do.

Chapter Two Questions

Question: Describe a time in your life when an offense from someone else led you to foster sin in your own heart. What was the result of that experience?

_____

_____

_____

_____

_____

_____

_____

_____

Question: Take an honest look at your life. Are there areas where sin has seeped into your lifestyle? What changes do you need to make?

_____

_____

_____

_____

_____

_____

_____

_____

_____

_____

_____

Action: Set aside some time to get away from external distractions, especially electronics and entertainment, as much as possible. Use this time to ask God to reveal any sin in your heart that needs to be removed. Allow Him to show you practical changes you can make to address sin and rise above temptation.

Chapter Two Notes

CHAPTER THREE

Forgiveness

"You'll never get involved in this church again."

My jaw dropped a little, and I stared blankly back at my friend and church leader. Hiding emotions is a skill lots of people fine-tune during adulthood, but my honesty always seems to get in the way. I tried to swallow the lump of humiliation in my throat.

When I had first started attending my beloved church, I was married to my first wife. I was a part of the worship team, a member of the choir, and a big contributor to Sunday-school discussions. I was getting ready to lead my own men's Bible study. And then my wife left me.

Like many people facing an unexpected separation, I desperately needed the support of my Christian brothers and sisters. I stepped away from my ministry for a while and got some counseling.

After my divorce was final, I was eager to start working for God again. That's when I was told that my time was over.

Opening Doors

The church I was in back then no longer holds the same position on divorced people, but the rejection stuck with me for a long time. Believe it or not, I had grown up with similar teachings about those whose marriages had ended through a divorce. I walked away understanding why God had closed the door for me. Sin had entered my life. I knew that I had to forgive the church leaders and move on.

Still, I couldn't shake the feeling that God had ministry plans for me. I told Him that if He ever gave me another opportunity to serve Him, I would pursue it without a question.

The next few years were a roller coaster of ups and downs in my walk with the Lord. When Word of Life Fellowship asked me to come on staff, I was honest with them. "I don't think that would work," I told them. "I'm divorced. I'm not worthy of that kind of service."

Their response surprised me. They said, "Let's let God decide if you're worthy or not."

This was the first time in a long time that God provided such an opportunity. I had been waiting for a cracked door, and He responded by blowing one wide open.

Once I joined the Word of Life team, I had a painful first couple of years. I was still straddling the line between wanting to be in ministry and thinking that I didn't deserve to be. But when you let God be in control, He asks you to surrender your plans.

God kept blessing me, guiding me, and providing for me

in ways I had never imagined possible. I finally decided to stop fighting Him. In my heart, I wondered if I would be staying at Word of Life for good.

Then the Lord opened the door for me to come back home. He knew that I had a daughter who needed me. Someone called and told me, "We want you to be the pastor of your dad's church."

Again, I responded, "I'm not qualified. I've made mistakes in the past."

Once again, the men of God assured me, "God will decide whether or not you're qualified. Let's at least take a chance."

Initially, the numbers at my father's church went down when I became the pastor. There were still folks who couldn't accept the fact that I was divorced. But after the early dip from 120 to 75 congregants, we began to grow. After just six years, we were pushing 550 to 600 people. Then God called me to an even greater opportunity.

When people asked me why I was making a change, I responded that I was in no place to question God's plans. When He puts something on my plate, I surrender to Him, period.

If the church I was at when I was first married had forgiven me for the divorce, who knows where I would be today. God used the pain and rejection caused by immature Christians to lead me to a new understanding.

I don't want to be like the pastor who told me that I could never serve again. I want to be a leader who knows how to love and forgive and who sets an example that others can follow. Even so, I struggle with forgiveness sometimes and am thankful that God is patient as we learn how to let go of offenses.

CONFLICT AND PRIVACY

As my church continued to grow, I was blessed with five amazing men who became my core army, a trusted pastoral staff. One of these men was exceptionally talented. I thought that he could be the lead pastor of his own church one day. He was a devoted friend, father, and coach who loved people in a way it was impossible to fake. I often discussed this with our discipleship pastor, who acted as a father figure to all of us budding young preachers.

At the time, my wife and I felt strongly that I was being called to leave my position as lead pastor and serve at Word of Life Fellowship as the Director of Advancement. One of the main reasons I felt so comfortable moving on was because of the promise I saw in this young pastor. I knew that the church would be in good hands if I turned over the reins.

At the time, the only people who knew about my transition were the discipleship pastor and the young preacher himself. We would have to keep the secret from the rest of our congregation for six months while we made important decisions. There were exciting moments during this period, but there were also times when I had difficulty letting go. The other pastors noticed and believed that I was still hanging on.

I was very pleased with how our church had grown since I had begun my ministry there. We had started a building campaign and raised all of the money we needed for a new auditorium with zero debt. Our numbers grew, our staff expanded, and we purchased six more acres of land next to the church for future expansion. We could use the space to accommodate our growing numbers, including a thriving children's ministry. I knew that God was setting us up for prosperity and continued growth.

At one point, I met with my discipleship pastor to discuss a concern I had about the young pastor. I knew that it needed to be addressed before he was asked to lead.

My discipleship pastor looked me in the eye. "Let me handle this," he said. "I have seen some of these things in him before, and it will give me a good opportunity to begin working seriously with him, especially with you transitioning out."

They had their meeting a few days later. From that day on, there was tension between the younger pastor and me. The truth is that I should have gone to the young pastor myself. He would have been able to understand the heart behind my concern. While my relationship with the young pastor has improved since then, it isn't what it used to be. I should not have involved someone else in our discussion.

When we go to someone privately, we gain that person's trust. When we involve someone else first, we are inviting suspicion.

MATTHEW 18 AND FORGIVENESS

When I think of Matthew 18, I know that there are some things I'm learning to do better, as well as others I still need to work on. Let's revisit the passage:

> *If your brother sins against you, go and tell him his fault, between you and him alone. If he listens to you, you have gained your brother. But if he does not listen, take one or two others along with you, that every charge may be established by the evidence of two or three witnesses. If he refuses to listen to them, tell it to the church. And if he refuses to listen even to the church, let him be to you as a Gentile and a tax collector.*
>
> *—Matthew 18:15–17*

When someone offends you, the first thing you're called to do is to keep the matter between the two of you. Too often, we try to build an army before we go to the person who hurt us. We feel like we need backup so we won't be alone in defending our position.

When we counsel couples who are about to get married, we always discuss this. It's important for spouses not to talk badly about each other to their families, friends, or co-workers. Young husbands and wives can become frustrated and feel the need to vent, but confiding in those who know both of them has its consequences.

Well-meaning family members and friends will probably take the side of the spouse to whom they're closest and develop a negative view of the other spouse. This can further exacerbate the issues between the two people in the marriage to the point where they're no longer working as a team.

In healthy marriages, hurt spouses go to their partners first. It's only when there is no resolution that they involve two or three witnesses who can help to give a voice to their struggles.

This is true in other relationships as well. We need to go to the individual first. If there is no resolution after that private discussion, we should bring along two or three witnesses. If there's still no resolution, we need to bring the matter to members of the spiritually mature church. There's no reason to discuss sins in front of the whole congregation or to make a public mockery of the person who offended us. Instead, we should bring the person into fellowship with the church as a whole with the intent of regaining our brother or sister. Our design should never be to hurt or embarrass anyone.

This is supposed to be an act of love. It's only after we have tried everything else that we should turn someone over to the consequences of his or her sin. The reason we have the other steps in place is that we often struggle with forgiveness.

GETTING HURT AGAIN

Warren Wiersbe once said, "When we start living in an atmosphere of humility and honesty, we must take some risks and expect some dangers. Unless humility and honesty result in forgiveness, relationships cannot be mended and strengthened."[6]

Wiersbe was saying that when we forgive people, we have to take the risk that we could be hurt again. The truth is that we probably will be. Sin is on the attack all of the time, and it's the nature of sin to destroy relationships. In order to make relationships work, we must take the risk that someone might hurt us a second time.

In Matthew 18:21, Peter asked Jesus, "Lord, how often will my brother sin against me, and I forgive him? As many as seven times?"

Jesus replied, "I do not say to you seven times, but seventy-seven times" (Matthew 18:22).

Peter actually thought that he was being generous. At the time, rabbis said that you could forgive someone who offended you up to three times.[7] Jesus, however, wanted us to know that there is no limit to forgiveness. As Christian brothers and sisters, we are to pour out forgiveness like water from an open spout on a scorching summer day.

Love keeps no record of wrongs, but it isn't blind. It calls out sin by coming alongside those who struggle and lifting them up in righteousness. If we love God the way we say we do, we will love our brothers and sisters with godly love.

We can't trust people if we don't understand that they love us. Our brothers and sisters won't be able to digest correction if they don't believe that we truly have their best interests at heart. Love is a critical part of being able to confront people well.

When we trust others, we begin to feel safe. When we love the way God loves, our barriers come down. We open ourselves up to hearing about our weaknesses and getting hurt again, but we also create the possibility that we could fully know and still completely love our Christian family.

THE UNGRATEFUL SERVANT

In Matthew 18:23–27, Jesus told us an important story about forgiveness:

> *Therefore the kingdom of heaven may be compared to a king who wished to settle accounts with his servants. When he began to settle, one was brought to him who owed him ten thousand talents. And since he could not pay, his master ordered him to be sold, with his wife and children and all that he had, and payment to be made. So the servant fell on his knees, imploring him, "Have patience with me, and I will pay you everything." And out of pity for him, the master of that servant released him and forgave him the debt.*

The servant in the passage owed a debt that was extremely high, and his master chose to forgive him the debt. I had to learn to accept the truth of God's forgiveness in my own life. I knew how much I owed Him, but I also needed to believe that God chose to forgive me anyway. Jesus made the ultimate sacrifice so that we could be forgiven. Sometimes it's hard to believe that Jesus really loves us that much. Accepting Jesus' love for us and His forgiveness also means that we need to extend that same forgiving spirit to those who offend us.

Unfortunately, many members of the church behave more like the forgiven servant did in Matthew 18:28–29:

But when that same servant went out, he found one of his fellow servants who owed him a hundred denarii, and seizing him, he began to choke him, saying, "Pay what you owe." So his fellow servant fell down and pleaded with him, "Have patience with me, and I will pay you."

The man whose master had forgiven him a large sum had little patience with his fellow servant, who owed him only a small sum. In fact, today it would equate to around $10 or $20. Instead of forgiving his fellow servant, "he went off and had the man thrown into prison until he could pay the debt" (Matthew 18:30 NIV). The ungrateful servant had clearly forgotten how much he had just been forgiven. His pride led him to believe that the small debt owed him was more important than the one he could never begin to pay back.

God forgives us for all things. As sinners, we deserve death and hell. But because of what Jesus did for us on the cross, we are rescued! We owe Him everything. When Jesus says that we need to forgive, He means that it's our turn. It may be hard for us, but it cost Jesus more. If we remember His sacrifice and our need for salvation, we'll be able to forgive people every time they wrong us.

FORGIVENESS AND OUR HEARTS

One of the most difficult things I have ever had to do was to go to my ex-wife and her new husband and ask for forgiveness. I asked him to pardon me for, of all things, hating him. The truth was that he had done one of the worst things in the world to me. He had torn my family apart. But I knew that if I didn't show him grace and forgiveness, he would never know the love of God.

Because I forgave him, our relationship changed. I no longer saw him as an enemy. We were able to communicate in our new roles, even though I had never wanted to be in that situation.

Many of us choose to separate from others because they hurt us and we can't take any more pain. Churches often divide because we want things our way or because we put our own convictions ahead of godly understanding.

There was an unhappy end to the ungrateful servant's story:

> *Then his master summoned him and said to him, "You wicked servant! I forgave you all that debt because you pleaded with me. And should not you have had mercy on your fellow servant, as I had mercy on you?" And in anger his master delivered him to the jailers, until he should pay all his debt.*
> **—Matthew 18:32–34**

When we don't forgive other people, we are essentially saying that God's forgiveness was not sufficient. True lovers of Christ forgive because they understand how much God has forgiven them. Love is not just a feeling; it's an action. We can show our love for Christ by forgiving as He does. We don't have a choice. We must forgive each other in order to grow, and doing so can bring rewards we never dreamed of.

When we invite Jesus into our lives, we must surrender entirely to Him. This includes learning to love like He loves and forgive like He forgives. When we forgive our brothers and sisters, we show the type of sacrificial love the world desperately needs.

Chapter Three Questions

Question: Have you experienced an offense that was difficult to forgive? How did your reluctance or refusal to forgive impact your relationship with God? How did it affect your life? Are you still hanging on to that offense?

_____

_____

_____

_____

_____

_____

_____

_____

Question: When you confront someone about his or her sin, do you do so with pride, arrogance, or anger? How do you think that attitude will affect the person you're confronting? What would be a better way to approach someone who has wronged you?

_____

_____

_____

_____

_____

_____

_____

_____

_____

_____

_____

Action: Whom do you need to forgive? In a journal or notebook, write a prayer expressing your choice to forgive this person. If appropriate and safe, pursue steps of reconciliation with this person.

Chapter Three Notes

Be Set Apart

I was up at Camp Beechpoint rolling up sleeping bags and zipping up knapsacks when a staff member from the housekeeping department mentioned something interesting.

"I don't know why it is," she said, "but we replace broomsticks all the time."

I looked up, amused. "Do you know boys?"

She was a little perplexed. "What are you talking about?"

"Well, my boys see a stick, and they don't care what's at the other end of it. They're using it as a sword."

She stared back at me. "Oh my goodness, now that you mention it, we are finding them broken in all the boys' cabins! But there's a sign up there that says, 'Do Not Use Broom!'"

I chuckled. "You're talking about boys. You just gave them a sign that says, 'Use the Broom!'"

THE LAW AND THE FLESH

As human beings, we know what happens when someone gives us a rule. We say things like, "Man, I can't do that? I'll show them!"

When we're not controlled by the Spirit, we're manipulated by our flesh, which makes us want to break the law. We have free will, and we want to be in control. Often the addition of rules causes more problems. It's never a good thing when the government makes more laws. It can actually lead to a higher crime rate. As a people, we need to be governed by the Spirit of truth rather than human regulations.

The Bible is a practical book that knows more about our own hearts than we do.

> *There is therefore now no condemnation for those who are in Christ Jesus. For the law of the Spirit of life has set you free in Christ Jesus from the law of sin and death. For God has done what the law, weakened by the flesh, could not do. By sending his own Son in the likeness of sinful flesh and for sin, he condemned sin in the flesh, in order that the righteous requirement of the law might be fulfilled in us, who walk not according to the flesh but according to the Spirit. For those who live according to the flesh set their minds on the things of the flesh, but those who live according to the Spirit set their minds on the things of the Spirit. For to set the mind on the flesh is death, but to set the mind on the Spirit is life and peace. For the mind that is set on the flesh is hostile to God, for it does not submit to God's law; indeed, it cannot. Those who are in the flesh cannot please God.*

You, however, are not in the flesh but in the Spirit, if in fact the Spirit of God dwells in you. Anyone who does not have the Spirit of Christ does not belong to him. But if Christ is in you, although the body is dead because of sin, the Spirit is life because of righteousness. If the Spirit of him who raised Jesus from the dead dwells in you, he who raised Christ Jesus from the dead will also give life to your mortal bodies through his Spirit who dwells in you.

So then, brothers, we are debtors, not to the flesh, to live according to the flesh. For if you live according to the flesh you will die, but if by the Spirit you put to death the deeds of the body, you will live. For all who are led by the Spirit of God are sons of God. For you did not receive the spirit of slavery to fall back into fear, but you have received the Spirit of adoption as sons, by whom we cry, "Abba! Father!" The Spirit himself bears witness with our spirit that we are children of God, and if children, then heirs—heirs of God and fellow heirs with Christ, provided we suffer with him in order that we may also be glorified with him.

—Romans 8:1–17

What does it mean to "live according to the flesh"? This means living in sin and trying to satisfy the desires of our human nature, such as greed and lust. It means committing misdeeds, such as theft and adultery. There's also worry, jealousy, lying, and gossip, which we tend to engage in more freely. And how about all of the idols we put above God in our lives? These could even be otherwise good things, such as family, school, or our jobs.

Sometimes as Christians, we seek to let the Spirit be our guide while the flesh remains our law. If our flesh wants to do something that goes against God's will, we find ways to twist His Word to say what we want it to say so we can justify our actions. When we do this, we're still living according to the flesh.

THE SPIRIT AND OUR FAMILIES

This is becoming a trend in churches today. I recently heard about an elder at a church near mine. He was a little concerned that his pastor was talking about grace all the time but never seemed to mention sin.

The elder pulled the pastor aside to make sure that he wasn't misinterpreting him. "You know, it seems like we talk about grace a lot here, but we never discuss the sins we're being forgiven of. How about, for example, homosexual marriage? Where do we stand on that?"

The pastor hesitated before replying, "Well, I believe in grace."

"Fine," the elder responded, "but I'm asking you about this particular issue, and I need an answer. Where does the church stand?"

He answered slowly, "I think it's open to interpretation."

The elder was saddened. "This is black and white," he said. "We know what God's Word says."

The elder ended up leaving the church because the pastor would not stand up for the truth in God's Word.

Sometimes it's smart to be open-minded, but it can lead to sin if what we're allowing is of the flesh and not the Spirit. If we believe that God is who He says He is, we will be filled with the Holy Spirit. The world will tell us that all kinds of sins are acceptable and that we can find ways to make them work within our relationship with God. Our modern world will tell us that it's okay to be a different type of person from who we were created to be, but that is a misinterpretation of grace.

God doesn't make mistakes. If He made you a man, He wants you to be a man. If He made you a woman, you are a woman created for His purposes. Period. When we begin to think that we could be happier otherwise, Satan is pleased that we have fallen into his trap.

Christ is the head of the church, and men are placed in authority over women. They shouldn't be dictators, but rather lead with gentleness. Wives are called to allow their husbands to lead with grace. When we follow God's plan for our families, we will be amazed by the results.

LEADING OUR FAMILIES

Believe it or not, what we are dealing with as a church today is not new. Rome was also experiencing the same problem: a misinterpretation. They were looking for more laws to define them. We usually prefer laws given by other people over the leading of the Spirit. We're afraid of what the Spirit might tell us if we choose to trust Him. Most of all, we're scared of what we'll have to give up.

The Spirit disciplines us when we fall away. Those of us who are parents understand this. We love our children even when we're disciplining them. Similarly, God disciplines us out of love when we fall into sin.

Pastors know that if we're leading our families biblically,

our home families and our church families are really the same thing. If we start to place our biological families ahead of the church, we begin to justify things that are not biblical.

If we aren't leading our children, how will we know how they fit into the church? As a church body, we need to help young people understand their unique roles. Are they excellent singers, or do they like to work with younger children? Maybe they are gifted woodworkers or enjoy cooking meals for the community.

I believe the reason so many of our youth end up leaving the church when they go to college is that we don't allow them to use their spiritual gifts. If they feel useful and needed, they'll find more meaning in the body of Christ.

There should be only three levels of priority for those of us who are believers: God, our brothers and sisters (including family, extended family, and the church), and ministry. Notice that your job is not on this list! Investing in your family at home as well as your spiritual family is more important to our heavenly Father than your career.

As a church, we need to give people purposeful roles in our community. It's not just the pastor who is in ministry. We are all a part of the same ministry in Christ.

THE LAW AND SIN

Romans 8:6 reminds us that "to set the mind on the flesh is death, but to set the mind on the Spirit is life and peace." The mind set on the flesh is hostile to God; it contradicts Him. As Christians, if we continue to allow the flesh to hold sway in an area of our lives, we will wrestle, some of us inwardly and some of us outwardly. If we are living according to the desires of the flesh, we cannot please God. Sin is sin, whether we like it or not.

At one point in my life, I was leading a youth group and was still struggling with pornography. The worst part about it was that I was looking at it on my dad's computer. I didn't want to watch it at home.

I tried to handle this sin on my own, but it was making me sick. The hardest day of my life came when I was convicted at a youth rally about my problem. Then I made an incredibly difficult decision. I made up my mind to tell my dad about my sin. I knew that I could no longer struggle in silence. I said, "Dad, I've been using your computer to sin. I need help."

My dad and I drove around quietly for an hour. Finally, he said, in his loving and gracious way, "Chip, is there nothing else?"

I was undone. "I can't be a youth leader anymore. I'm struggling with pornography. I can't do this without someone else on my side."

My dad lovingly put his arms around me. "Son, I knew you were struggling. I was just waiting for you to come to me."

What should we do when we wrestle with sin? The Bible says that we need to be filled with the Spirit. As a pastor, I had an entire pastoral team to hold me accountable. I knew that they weren't going to judge me, and I knew that my congregation wouldn't, either. They were going to strengthen me because that's what we do in the Spirit. God tells us that we all struggle in the flesh, but we can work things out if we go to Him.

We are not in control of the Spirit; we simply need to allow Him to work. We need to surrender our flesh and our identity fully to God instead of hanging on to them for ourselves, as if we know better than He does.

Romans 8:14 tells us that "all who are led by the Spirit of God are sons of God." Romans 8:17 continues, "...if children, then heirs—heirs of God and fellow heirs with Christ, provided we suffer with him in order that we may also be glorified with him." As Christians, we are going to suffer so that Christ may be glorified in us. We need to bear our burdens, just as He did. If we remain in the Spirit instead of living for our flesh, the suffering will work out for His glory.

TRUST HIM

Romans 8:9 says, "You, however, are not in the flesh but in the Spirit, if in fact the Spirit of God dwells in you. Anyone who does not have the Spirit of Christ does not belong to him." When we are living in the Spirit, we no longer have to follow the directions of our flesh. We have escaped the rule of our sinful selves and can begin living under the law of peace and righteousness.

My daughter spoke to me recently. She'd had a really special God moment she wanted to share.

"You know, Dad," she said, "I finally figured it out. God wants me to trust Him. It doesn't matter what other people think."

I was impressed. "Who told you that?"

"Nobody," she said. "I was just reading God's Word, and the Holy Spirit was telling me."

When we read God's Word, we get a glimpse of who He is and what He has in store for us. God fills us up with the Holy Spirit until we are overflowing. The more we allow the Holy Spirit to fill us up and pour into every area of our lives, the less likely we are to sin.

Chapter Four Questions

Question: Are there any indicators that you are living more by the flesh than by the Spirit in any area of your life? Why do you think you are choosing the flesh in that area?

_____

_____

_____

_____

_____

_____

_____

_____

Question: Is there a habitual sin in your life that you are struggling to overcome? Why is it so hard to give it up? Write a prayer acknowledging this sin before God.

_____

_____

_____

_____

_____

_____

_____

_____

_____

_____

_____

Action: Choose a godly person you trust to share your struggle with sin. Invite that person to hold you accountable and walk with you through the struggle. If you need more than one person, invite more people to come alongside you as you face your sin and grow in the Spirit.

Chapter Four Notes

_____

_____

_____

_____

_____

_____

_____

_____

_____

_____

_____

_____

_____

_____

_____

_____

_____

_____

_____

Be Kind

These days, kindness is as trendy as a top-ten hit. The "kindness movement" seeks to emphasize the power of kindness through education and awareness.

Kind Bars are popular healthy snacks in my house. The company has sought to encourage kindness throughout the nation by allowing folks to visit their website and recognize others who have done kind things. They then thank the purveyors of kindness by sending them treats, such as snacks and gift cards. Each year, they give away thousands of dollars in free merchandise in the name of rewarding kind acts.[8]

Ellen DeGeneres is a popular figure who constantly talks about kindness on her show. Her loyal viewers are encouraged to purchase "Kind Boxes" that contain brands and products sold by companies that give to charity and positively impact the community.[9]

The kindness movement promotes some beautiful Christian values. It encourages folks to respect each other and not to bully people for being different. The part I struggle with is that the movement is not coming from the church, but from nonbelieving individuals who see others being mistreated or oppressed and inherently know that it's wrong. They see injustice and seek ways to lift up those who feel beaten down. As Christians, we should be the ones modeling kindness to a suffering world.

KINDNESS AND COACHING

Ephesians 4:32 tells us to "be kind to one another, tenderhearted, forgiving one another, as God in Christ forgave you." Kindness is described here not only as something we do, but also as something we evolve into being. God calls us to be tenderhearted, meaning that we should have soft hearts toward our brothers and sisters. We need to learn to forgive others when they offend us like Christ forgives us.

As a coach, I find that being kind often translates into respecting my junior athletes as individuals. I often ask myself if I'm trying to make the kids more like Christ or more like me. This helps to change my perspective. Suddenly, winning and losing aren't as important anymore. I often hear from others that "we still have to win." In my experience, the more I invest in the kids, the more we end up winning.

When we watch coaches on TV, we may notice that the camera tends to focus on those who are screaming and bullying, because they will have the greatest interest for the audience. There are no cameras on the coach who is gentle and tenderhearted. As Christians, we don't need that kind of attention. Jesus deserves to be front and center. We don't need to be on camera.

Sometimes we need to yell in order to get our kids' attention. They may be ignoring us when there's something important they need to change. If we're yelling for the right reason, it may not be sinful, but it's easy to lose control of the way we yell. When we lose control, we can get off track and sin against our kids.

Some of us need to take this to heart when it comes to our children. We can get carried away and end up wounding their spirits. Saying something sternly in a firm voice is often all they need. They know that what they're doing is wrong. The next time you're tempted to raise your voice or use harsh language, consider whether or not it's necessary. Many times, the only thing you need is a little serious honesty.

KINDNESS AND CONFRONTATION

As we discuss the Matthew 18 principle, we must remember how critical kindness is at every step. Instead of harboring anger or bitterness toward those who have offended us, we are to approach them in kindness and love. The verses leading up to Ephesians 4:32 are also extremely important in shaping the attitude we should have when confronting fellow believers:

Therefore, having put away falsehood, let each one of you speak the truth with his neighbor, for we are members one of another. Be angry and do not sin; do not let the sun go down on your anger, and give no opportunity to the devil.
—Ephesians 4:25–27

Notice that the Bible is not telling us not to be angry. Many believe that Christians should be docile saints who are never offended at anything. However, there are times when our anger is appropriate. It's a natural reaction to hurt that can help us to protect ourselves from further mistreatment. However, we are instructed not to remain angry for a long time, as this will give the devil an opportunity. Another translation says that it will "give the devil a foothold" (Ephesians 4:27 NIV).

Following the Matthew 18 steps when we're angry is important because when we remain angry with someone, we give Satan a step up in our lives. A foothold is literally a place that can securely support your foot while you're climbing. When we refuse to forgive, the devil is getting a nice, snug spot where he can rest his foot as he tries to gain victory over our lives. We need to let our brothers and sisters know when they hurt us and give them a chance to apologize. If we don't, we run the risk of holding on to the pain and allowing Satan a chance to gain control.

Let the thief no longer steal, but rather let him labor, doing honest work with his own hands, so that he may have something to share with anyone in need. Let no corrupting talk come out of your mouths, but only such as is good for building up, as fits the occasion, that it may give grace to those who hear. And do not grieve the Holy Spirit of God, by whom you were sealed for the day of redemption. Let all bitterness and wrath and anger and clamor and slander be put away from you, along with all malice. Be kind to one another, tenderhearted, forgiving one another, as God in Christ forgave you.

—Ephesians 4:28–32

What we see here is a call to give up our old ways and begin using our time productively so that we can give to those in need. This is good practical and spiritual advice. It can help us to avoid the idleness and loneliness that can lead to sin and depression. Folks who spend their time doing useful things and giving generously are usually much happier!

We are also called to get rid of negative and violent talk. We shouldn't let our anger control us or lash out in fits of rage. All of this is destructive when it comes to relationships. How do you think nonbelievers feel when they hear Christians speaking with hostility or contempt? Do you think that sets a good example of Jesus' love? No, it doesn't.

As followers of Christ, we are to be gentle, affectionate, and loving. This is harder for some of us than for others. We need to put ourselves in other people's shoes, consider their best interests, and respect them. This can be particularly difficult after someone has hurt us badly, but a loving response to offense gives a powerful testimony of Christ's love to a world desperate for hope and reconciliation.

AMBASSADORS OF CHRIST

The Bible calls us to be "ambassadors for Christ" (2 Corinthians 5:20). We are meant to act as representatives and promoters of our Father in heaven. Sometimes we hear of folks who sell products being ambassadors of their parent companies. This means that their speech, their dress, and even their social media presence seek to represent the best of what the brand has to offer.

First John 3:1 says:

> *See what kind of love the Father has given to us, that we should be called children of God; and so we are. The reason why the world does not know us is that it did not know him.*

We are called to be children of God. What a cool promise! The reason the world doesn't understand us is that it doesn't know God the way we do.

My daughter, Emily, is twenty-two years old now. But I remember something that happened when she was only about eight or nine years old that speaks volumes to the importance of the way we live as Christians.

She had just seen me preach a message about how people won't know the love of Christ if they don't see it in His followers. Other people can only be sure of our relationship with God if they can see the fruit of that relationship, including gentleness, patience, and kindness. After the sermon, Emily wanted to talk to me in person.

"Dad, I've been spending a lot of time with my friend who says they know Jesus," she said. "But their life isn't telling me that they do. They swear a lot and live their life however they want. I just don't see Jesus. Do you think they are really saved?"

It was a tough question for me to answer. We want to believe that everyone we know is going to heaven and will have eternal life, but in reality, that's not always the case. Even Satan and the demons know that there is one God (James 2:19).

I don't know whether or not this person had truly been rescued from sin by Jesus, but what I told my daughter was that others wouldn't be attracted to Jesus based on what they saw in this individual's life. In fact, that person was doing the work of our enemy.

CHILDREN OF RIGHTEOUSNESS

As children of God, it's critical that we set an example of righteousness. This involves standing up for things that are morally right and justifiable. When we practice the holy attributes of God, we are setting a good example. Our righteousness should mirror that of the One to whom we gave our lives.

First John 3:4–6 tells us:

Everyone who makes a practice of sinning also practices lawlessness; sin is lawlessness. You know that he appeared in order to take away sins, and in him there is no sin. No one who abides in him keeps on sinning; no one who keeps on sinning has either seen him or known him.

When God called us to be His children, the gift came with responsibility. Sin is the piece of our lives that separates us from God, but His love draws us in. If we continue to sin and act with cruelty toward one another, we aren't reflecting Christ to the world. Our mission should be to model His holiness, kindness, and patience. We will fail from time to time, but we are commanded to keep striving.

KINDNESS AND SIN IN OTHERS

Someone once asked me, "If someone is a lesbian, can she be saved?"

This has typically been a difficult question for the church to answer. My response is usually to ask, "So, if someone lies every day, do you think that person can be saved?"

The answer is, of course, yes. We are all sinners who struggle and desperately need a Savior. Both lying and sexual sins are unholy in God's eyes, but Christians don't tend to view people in that light. Many people in the church struggle with different kinds of sin, such as gossiping or selfishness, yet we rarely question whether or not these folks know the Lord. But for some reason, when we see people walking in confusion about their sexual identity, we automatically assume that they don't know Christ.

Jesus paid the price for all sin and rescued us from it. We have only to accept that gift, and Jesus offers it to every kind of sinner. Many people made a decision to follow Christ in their lives at some point but eventually walked away. I believe the reason is that no one in the church encouraged them or came along to help them through the process. As ambassadors, we need to guide people on their journey and show them what they're missing.

When Jesus met the woman at the well (John 4), He didn't shame her even though He knew that she had been living an immoral life. He decided to see her as the person God created, rather than a woman struggling with sin. As Christians, it's our job to mirror Christ's love. We need to see others as Christ does, not as the sum of their fleshly mistakes.

Second Corinthians 3:18 reassures us that "we all, with unveiled face, beholding the glory of the Lord, are being transformed into the same image from one degree of glory to another. For this comes from the Lord who is the Spirit."

Those whose eyes have been opened are being transformed into the image of Christ. It may take longer for some of us to get there than others. If someone is still living a lifestyle of sin, God may be in the process of working in that person's heart.

My biggest struggle has always been with lust and pornography. Satan knows this, and he tries to trap me during my weakest moments. When I'm struggling, isolated, or not spending time in the Word, he knows that he can throw those darts of temptation at me. Images will start to show up on my phone that I haven't seen for weeks or months. During my most vulnerable times, I might even click on one. Does that mean that I'm not a Christian? No, it means that I'm a Christian who gave into sin.

We've all seen people who have wrestled with substance abuse, such as alcohol or smoking, in the past, and now they don't struggle at all anymore. They left it behind and never touched it again. We've also seen people who grapple with their sin for years. It doesn't mean that they don't love the Lord.

As a Christian, I don't consider it my job to try to transform people through persuasion. Rather, they need to be encouraged by seeing Jesus through me. We won't be completely transformed until we go to be with our Savior for eternity.

In my previous church, we had a person come to our services, and at first, he was dressed in men's clothing. Then I noticed that he started wearing earrings and other feminine accessories. Finally, one day, he came to church dressed head-to-toe in women's clothing.

After the service, this person asked if he could speak to me. I was a bit surprised when he asked me if he was still allowed to attend our worship meetings.

"Absolutely," I said.

He looked around. "What about what the people here will think about me?"

I turned toward them. "It doesn't matter what they think. You need to be here because you need to hear God's Word."

I think the truth is that this person was challenging me and wanted to see how I would respond to the question.

Over time, the individual stopped coming to church altogether. While he was gutsy enough to challenge me on some issues, I don't think that he was ready for God to challenge him. But he was more than welcome to come to church.

I believe that when God looked at this person, He saw the brokenness of someone who had either walked away from Him or never had a relationship with Him. The only way people will ever find their Savior is if we love them the same way Christ loved us when we were still lost. We are called not to judge, but to view others the way He does.

A NEW CREATION

From now on, therefore, we regard no one according to the flesh. Even though we once regarded Christ according to the flesh, we regard him thus no longer. Therefore, if anyone is in Christ, he is a new creation. The old has passed away; behold, the new has come. All this is from God, who through Christ reconciled us to himself and gave us the ministry of reconciliation; that is, in Christ God was reconciling the world to himself, not counting their trespasses against them, and entrusting to us the message of reconciliation. Therefore, we are ambassadors for Christ, God making his appeal through us. We implore you on behalf of Christ, be reconciled to God.
—2 Corinthians 5:16–20

When people are saved, they may look and act the same as they did before. You still see your old friend, your child, or your acquaintance. But the reality is that when someone is saved, he or she is a new spiritual creation. The old has passed away. As Christians, we must be ambassadors of Christ's love. We can choose to see sinners as people who don't yet know Christ or are still growing in Him. We can choose to believe that God is doing a powerful work in their lives.

Chapter Five Questions

Question: Is your life characterized by kindness? When people who aren't believers encounter you or observe the way you live, do they see a kindness that draws them in?

_____

_____

_____

_____

_____

_____

_____

_____

Question: What example do nonbelievers or struggling Christians see when they look at your life? Does your example testify of the goodness and grace of Jesus?

_____

_____

_____

_____

_____

_____

_____

_____

_____

_____

Action: Who in your life needs a tangible representation of God's love and kindness? Ask God to show you something intentional you can do for that person to show God's love and brighten his or her life.

Chapter Five Notes

_____

_____

_____

_____

_____

_____

_____

_____

_____

_____

_____

_____

_____

_____

_____

_____

Be Encouraged

It was the kind of morning many pastors dream about. I went out to my mailbox and lifted the lid. There, thrillingly, was a check for a considerable amount of money from one of our members.

We had always envisioned finishing up one of our children's ministry areas, and my imagination was doing some interior design. New floorboards, finger painting tables, and custom sound systems were checkering through our current space and inspiring all of our tiniest believers.

Then I remembered that I had gotten a call from the health department earlier that week. They had asked me to come into their office. The birdies of excitement twittering around my head took a perch.

The health department doesn't usually ask you to visit in person. I had to be escorted in and out, just in case I was some sort of troublemaker. When I was ushered into the office of the inspector, he began to rub his leg. His cold stare let me know that I wasn't there to shoot the breeze with him. "So, how many people go to your church?" he asked.

Something told me to go with a conservative estimate. "Around 500."

He looked straight at me and took a deep breath. "Your church is too large. You're going to have to put that well in."

I straightened my back, suddenly realizing what the check I had gotten that morning was for. I was going to have to do the rest of the work to get this well done.

My relationship with this particular health employee had never been easy. From the first time he came to visit, he seemed to be looking for things that were wrong with our building. Each time he came out, he mentioned to me that he wasn't a believer. I realized that I had a unique opportunity to commend faith in God to him.

"What are you going to do?" he asked. "You've got a church of 500 people. You're going to have to promise me that you'll get me that money by the end of the month."

I said, "Actually, it isn't going to work that way. This morning, I went to the mailbox, and there was a check. God knew that I was coming here today and would need a way to pay for this."

His face immediately brightened. This man, who was challenging my faith and doubting my congregation, got a miracle he never expected. That's what is known as encouragement.

WELLSPRING OF ENCOURAGEMENT

Looking into Scripture, we see how critical it is for us to encourage one another daily and also those who don't know the Lord. We never know what the outcome will be. Someone could be listening to your testimony and thinking, *"I'm so glad you said that! Something just like that happened to me."*

> *Therefore, brothers, since we have confidence to enter the holy places by the blood of Jesus, by the new and living way that he opened for us through the curtain, that is, through his flesh, and since we have a great priest over the house of God, let us draw near with a true heart in full assurance of faith, with our hearts sprinkled clean from an evil conscience and our bodies washed with pure water. Let us hold fast the confession of our hope without wavering, for he who promised is faithful. And let us consider how to stir up one another to love and good works, not neglecting to meet together, as is the habit of some, but encouraging one another, and all the more as you see the Day drawing near.*
> **—Hebrews 10:19–25**

Something recently happened in our local school district that could have caused great discouragement to our church. We were basically told that our pastoral staff was no longer welcome there. We could undoubtedly have become disheartened and accepted defeat, but we remembered that Jesus said, "In the world you will have tribulation. But take heart; I have overcome the world" (John 16:33). So, we did the only thing we knew to do. The brothers and sisters prayed, and we asked God for a different type of opportunity.

Guess what happened the next week. The schools suddenly had a need for new baseball and basketball coaches, and we had people who could easily supply their needs. God can always provide the way.

Throughout the Bible, we see fantastic stories about how the faith of one person changed history. Imagine what the strength of many Christians can do!

Discouragement pushes us away from God, but encouragement draws us closer to Him and to each other. When we're discouraged, we tend to go into isolation, which can lead to depression. Loneliness creates a downward spiral that makes us feel unworthy of love and acceptance. It can lead to pain, embarrassment, and nasty habits. Overeating, overspending, and media outlets become terrible substitutes for the human fellowship we so badly need. Eventually, we become so comfortable in our defeat and self-pity that nothing else even seems natural.

On the other hand, when we're encouraged by someone, we can pop right out of whatever funk we're in. Every time I tell a fellow Christian that I'm discouraged about something, the weight seems to lift off my chest. Once I talk about my fears out loud, I realize that they're not as monstrous as I imagined. Instead of trudging further into a tunnel of loss and shame, I'm able to see bright hope for the future. I know that God has already taken care of my problem before anything new has happened.

PROMISES AND FULFILLMENT

Oftentimes, though we don't like to admit it, the reason we become discouraged is that we're struggling in sin. God forgives us completely, but we continue to wallow as though nothing better is possible.

> *For if we go on sinning deliberately after receiving the knowledge of the truth, there no longer remains a sacrifice for sins, but a fearful expectation of judgment, and a fury of fire that will consume the adversaries. Anyone who has set aside the law of Moses dies without mercy on the evidence of two or three witnesses. How much worse punishment, do you think, will be deserved by the one who has trampled underfoot the Son of God, and has profaned the blood of the covenant by which he was sanctified, and has outraged the Spirit of grace? For we know him who said, "Vengeance is mine; I will repay." And again, "The Lord will judge his people." It is a fearful thing to fall into the hands of the living God.*
> *—Hebrews 10:26–31*

It can be discouraging when we're still living in sin. We don't realize that we don't need to carry that burden anymore. The problem is that we don't truly believe that God forgave us, and we're drawn back into our old vices. Sometimes we're waiting for God to take care of our needs, but He is holding back because we're not being obedient. We also need to remember to thank God for where we are right now. Worrying is a sin. We need to be grateful for the blessings we already have, small and large.

Tony Evans talks about this best when he says that "there is a gap between God's promises and fulfillment."[10] If we shrink back because we're in a discouraging situation, we lengthen the time between God's promise and His fulfillment.

Think about that for a moment. The best example I can give of this is Job. He had friends who told him that he must have been suffering because of some unconfessed sin, but he didn't give into discouragement and beat himself up or start sinning. Instead, he believed that his entire struggle was part of God's plan.

We are not called to believe in God just so we can get what we want. That's the prosperity gospel. We are called to obey God by giving Him all that we have and are. There will be a reward, but it probably won't be a new house or car.

If you believe and God doesn't give you what you want, it's because you're telling Him what you deserve instead of letting Him give you what He desires you to have. When we are edified by the body of Christ through encouragement, we can obey God without question, even if there are things we seem to lack. When our friends discourage us, we're more tempted to give up and make bad decisions. These are the types of voices we need to ignore.

ENCOURAGE ONE ANOTHER DAILY

Living together isn't easy, is it? Even so, the Bible calls us not to tear each other apart or avoid each other, but to lift one another up as often as possible. Hebrews 3:13 tells us to "encourage one another daily, as long as it is called 'Today,' so that none of you may be hardened by sin's deceitfulness" (NIV).

There will come a time when there won't be any more days, but as long as there are, we must encourage each other so that we won't fall into sin. Most of the time, the world can be a discouraging place. When we are not being lifted up by our brothers and sisters, we'll be tempted to find comfort in the wrong places.

Satan actually has some very clever ways of distracting us when we're not being edified by the body of Christ. While they may not be sinful, networks like CNN and Fox News can be quite negative. Whichever side we're on, they suck us in with narratives in which there are clear villains and heroes. When our side isn't winning, we become frustrated and vexed. We think about all of the problems in the world and who we think is responsible for creating them.

Social media can also bring us into a sphere where we create deceitful stories about our lives. We show others snippets of our existence that will make them jealous. In return, we covet what they have and try to compete. We criticize what other people say and what they look like. Our hearts are becoming hardened without us even realizing it.

The media focuses on negative things because that's what sells, but God implores us to use our stories to encourage each other. You never know whom you could end up reaching.

ENCOURAGEMENT AND WORK

I once read an article about the "winning-est" girls' softball team in Michigan, where we lived at the time. They had won several state championships for consecutive years but then had to shut down their team. Why? The girls didn't want to work anymore. Michigan was thinking about cutting some baseball and softball programs, and their football teams kept getting smaller. The reason was disheartening: kids were losing interest in putting in the effort. They just wanted to win without doing the work.

As parents, we do our children a disservice when we fight their battles for them instead of letting them go through disappointments and challenges. Do you want your children to succeed in life? Do you want them to be set apart and exemplary? Then teach them to persevere through difficulties. They will develop character, grit, and courage, and they will give their peers something to think about.

The same is true in our relationship with God. We must be willing to work to get to know Him. We have to take time every day to learn what His Word says and talk to Him about what's in our hearts. We have to put Him before everything else, including our families. Once we do, everything else will fall in line. In our spiritual lives, we can only go forward or backward; we can't remain neutral.

ENCOURAGING EACH OTHER

Colossians 3:16 says, "Let the word of Christ dwell in you richly, teaching and admonishing one another in all wisdom, singing psalms and hymns and spiritual songs, with thankfulness in your hearts to God."

Encouraging one another is about more than just saying, "Hey, you look nice today." It's about helping your brothers' and sisters' souls to their feet. Ask them, "What are you going through?" or "How can I pray for you?" You have no idea how much you might help them to succeed in their spiritual journey.

I could have been discouraged when I faced my church's problem with the water supply. Instead, I prayed, and I thanked God for providing for us. When it came to our local schools, we sought God first. We decided to trust Him, and He gave us an opportunity to serve our enemies in love.

For you yourselves are fully aware that the day of the Lord will come like a thief in the night. While people are saying, "There is peace and security," then sudden destruction will come upon them as labor pains come upon a pregnant woman, and they will not escape. But you are not in darkness, brothers, for that day to surprise you like a thief. For you are all children of light, children of the day. We are not of the night or of the darkness.
—1 Thessalonians 5:2–5

As Christians, we know that the end will draw near one day. We can see some of the signs emerging already. There's a lot of talk of peace and a one-world government. Half of our country is against Israel, and half of us support them.

But we can be encouraged by the fact that Jesus is coming again. We will not have to face what nonbelievers will. All of the battles we may win or lose here will fade, but our Savior will live forever.

As the church, we are a family and the body of Christ. The power of the Holy Spirit is working in us and through us. When the Bible tells us to encourage one another, it's not just a saying. We need to strengthen each other as we walk with the Lord, because He is coming again.

Chapter Six Questions

Question: Describe a time when something deeply encouraging happened to you. How did you see God's heart reflected in that experience?

_____

_____

_____

_____

_____

_____

_____

_____

Question: Do discouraging circumstances ever bring you to a place of doubting God's promises and His goodness? How does the story of Job in the Bible affect your view of your circumstances and your view of God?

_____

_____

_____

_____

_____

_____

_____

_____

_____

Action: For one week, choose to fill your life with and spread encouragement. Avoid social media, discouraging news outlets, and entertainment that brings you down. Fill your life with uplifting content, messages, and experiences. (This doesn't mean that you should ignore difficult situations as they come up.) Intentionally speak uplifting words to the people in your life. What changes do you notice in your outlook and energy at the end of the week?

Chapter Six Notes

CHAPTER SEVEN

Causes and Cure for Conflict

Conflict is all around us. We get irritated in traffic, peeved at our bosses, and frustrated with our families. We think that we know better than someone else, who also has an unwavering position. What is the real source of all the conflict we see as Christians? Is it the weather, our nature, or our diet?

The Bible has a different explanation:

> *What causes quarrels and what causes fights among you? Is it not this, that your passions are at war within you? You desire and do not have, so you murder. You covet and cannot obtain, so you fight and quarrel. You do not have, because you do not ask. You ask and do not receive, because you ask wrongly, to spend it on your passions.*
> **—James 4:1–3**

The Bible is clear about the roots of our conflict. We want things that other people have, so we fight with everything

105

we've got. Our own desires bring us to blows with people with whom we used to live at peace.

All of this fighting is fruitless. Nothing good comes of it. On top of that, James points out that some of us don't have what we want simply because we're not asking for it. Are you having trouble paying the bills? Do your kids need braces? Are you wondering if you'll ever be able to retire? Believe it or not, God knows about those things.

Jesus said, "Look at the birds of the air: they neither sow nor reap nor gather into barns, and yet your heavenly Father feeds them. Are you not of more value than they?" (Matthew 6:26). God can provide for your needs, and all you have to do is ask Him. When He doesn't supply what you want, it's time to ask yourself a few questions.

Are you asking because you want more than what you need? Is what you're asking for a luxury or a necessity? Is there a way you can use more of what God gives you to provide for the needs of those who are less fortunate?

James 4 reminds us that God cares about our motives. When you're asking Him for something, think about why you want it. If your reasons are selfish, don't get angry about your unanswered prayers and take it out on others. Coveting won't provide you with anything but bitterness. Instead, consider how you can be a blessing to those who need you. God will provide you with what you need to serve others.

Going toe to toe with others because of our egotistical desires never ends well. James 4:4 indicates the sorry end we'll face when it says, "You adulterous people! Do you not know that friendship with the world is enmity with God?

Therefore whoever wishes to be a friend of the world makes himself an enemy of God."

Wanting the little bit of pleasure the world can give is more than just an irritation to God; it makes us His enemies. As Christians, that is not somewhere we want to be. The same passage, however, tells us where we can find the solution.

THE CURE FOR CONFLICT

Or do you suppose it is to no purpose that the Scripture says, "He yearns jealously over the spirit that he has made to dwell in us"? But he gives more grace. Therefore it says, "God opposes the proud but gives grace to the humble."
—James 4:5–6

Here we see two conflicting spirits. Our own human spirits are proud, jealous, and quarrelsome. We always want more and become enraged when others get what we think we deserve. By contrast, the Holy Spirit is full of grace. He loves to forgive us even though we don't deserve it. God is against those who are proud but offers grace to the humble.

Do you make an effort to lower your importance in your own eyes? This can be especially difficult if you're accomplished in some area or if God has blessed you with a lot of resources. It's essential to cultivate humility in your heart because God is on your side when you're humble, not when you're proud. Make an effort to appreciate other people's gifts, especially when others are talented in areas you are not. Remind yourself that God is the One who gave you whatever you have; you are not the author of it. If you choose to be humble, God will lift you up.

JUSTICE, NOT JUDGMENT

Humbling ourselves is hard. It's in our human nature to seek our own glory, but pride sets us against God. The Bible calls us to surrender to God and resist the devil:

> *Submit yourselves therefore to God. Resist the devil, and he will flee from you. Draw near to God, and he will draw near to you. Cleanse your hands, you sinners, and purify your hearts, you double-minded. Be wretched and mourn and weep. Let your laughter be turned to mourning and your joy to gloom. Humble yourselves before the Lord, and he will exalt you.*
> **—James 4:7–10**

Are you tempted to envy your brother? Are you angry because someone was promoted over you? Do you think it's time to go to war with an individual who did great damage to your life?

The Bible tells us to wash our hands and purify our hearts. When we resist the devil, he will flee from us. This is a wonderful promise! We don't have to give in to our desires to one-up our brothers. There's no need to fight and scream because we were wronged or mistreated. If we can hold out against our desires to do these things, we have won. The devil will eventually take a bus downtown when he realizes that he can't get a hold of us.

This is a call to obedience and to remove the dirt from our lives. We're also given the promise of the reward for humility. We may not feel special at first, but God will see our humble hearts and lift us up in due time.

Do you dream of getting promoted? Find out if there's work you can do that no one else wants to touch. Are you looking for a better marriage? Admit your flaws and shortcomings to your spouse. Humbling yourself can lead to great rewards. It will not go unnoticed by your heavenly Father.

SLANDER AND BOASTING

James goes on to address the way we treat one another:

Do not speak evil against one another, brothers. The one who speaks against a brother or judges his brother, speaks evil against the law and judges the law. But if you judge the law, you are not a doer of the law but a judge. There is only one lawgiver and judge, he who is able to save and to destroy. But who are you to judge your neighbor?
—James 4:11–12

Slandering and judging your neighbor can be detrimental to a humble spirit. Slander is when we make false statements that damage someone else's reputation. Many of us wouldn't slander someone in a public space, such as church or a PTA meeting, but how often do we do this in casual conversation?

We may think that we're sharing a juicy bit of information or passing along a concern, but the reality is that we like the way we feel when we share it. We enjoy making ourselves look good by contrast.

The Bible tells us that when we judge our neighbors, we're sitting in judgment on God's law itself. We don't have the right to determine what other people's sins or intentions are. Invariably, God will judge the slanderer instead. Therefore, we must learn to go to other people in love when there is a problem.

This same passage warns us about another prideful action: boasting.

> Come now, you who say, "Today or tomorrow we will go into such and such a town and spend a year there and trade and make a profit"—yet you do not know what tomorrow will bring. What is your life? For you are a mist that appears for a little time and then vanishes. Instead you ought to say, "If the Lord wills, we will live and do this or that." As it is, you boast in your arrogance. All such boasting is evil. So whoever knows the right thing to do and fails to do it, for him it is sin.
>
> **—James 4:13–17**

When you think of boasting, what kinds of conversations come into your head? Maybe it's someone at a party talking about how much money he makes or a straight-A student lording her successes over her classmates. We rarely think of making plans for going places or doing business as boasting. The problem isn't that we're thinking ahead; it's that we aren't thanking God when we do. Every time we make plans to improve our lives in some way, it's important to remember that God is the ultimate Source. If He grants us tomorrow and gives us the means, we will enjoy the blessings He provides.

In verse 14, James is asking us a philosophical question: "What is your life?" We are only here for a brief time. We need to keep an eternal perspective. The things that truly matter will last forever.

HUMBLE GREATNESS

Do you consider yourself humble? Who would you say is in control of your life? A sure-fire way to remain humble is to remind yourself who gave you your gifts and resources in the first place. It's all from God. When you keep that in mind, you can do nothing but serve Him with all you have, and that's a formula for eternal blessing.

Chapter Seven Questions

Question: Have you ever held a grudge against God when He didn't answer a selfish prayer? What do prayers focused on selfish gain reveal about your motives and the position of your heart? Do you make an effort to lower your importance in your own eyes? How is that reflected in your life?

_____

_____

_____

_____

_____

_____

_____

Question: Do you struggle to celebrate the wins in other people's lives? Do you envy what they have? If so, what do you think is at the root of this discontent?

_____

_____

_____

_____

_____

_____

_____

_____

_____

_____

Action: What is something you can do in your life to grow in humility? Think of the thing you want to do least in the world. Commit to doing that task as an exercise in humility. Look for opportunities to serve others and put others' needs before your own. Choose something specific and put it into practice.

Chapter Seven Notes

Change the Play

One night a few years ago, I was coaching a football team that wasn't particularly strong, but it was better than the team we were playing. We were winning handily, and we decided to bring our second string out to finish up the game. Rich, who later became quite a good friend, was coaching the other team.

During the huddle, our backup quarterback decided to change the play. The next thing I knew, with only two minutes left in the game, he pulled a ball out from the running back and tossed a bomb into the endzone. We caught it and scored. The kids were thrilled, but to the other coaches, it looked like we were running up the score.

I had been on the other side of this story many times, and I knew how opposing coaches were feeling. I could see them beginning to boil over. As soon as the clock expired, they sent their head coach out to the field. Our head coach, Brian, went out to meet him. He tried to explain what happened.

The head coach started saying more than he should, and I walked onto the field. I was ready to go to battle but had to remember that I was also the pastor in the community. We exchanged words, and Rich dragged his coach away to the bus. I realized that I had made a mistake in the things I said. Realizing my mistake, I went and found Rich on the bus and apologized.

A few months later, I met Rich at a football conference. Amazingly enough, I discovered that he was also a pastor. I encouraged him and his family to become a part of our church, but he ended up taking a job with a different congregation.

I stayed in touch with him and checked in regularly to see how I could encourage him. Over time, Rich ran into some conflict with the lead pastor because of the way he was handling people within the church. He confronted the pastor biblically, but the pastor turned on him, and everything changed. This put Rich in a tough spot. He knew that he needed to go, but he had invested so much time and energy in a community he loved. After several months, I again asked Rich to consider coming and serving with us so that he could find rest and healing.

After Rich had been on staff with us for six months, he asked me if he should apply for a job as a head football coach in a town that was a long drive from our church. I said "no" without even listening to him.

I could see Rich's face drop and heard the disappointment in his voice. All he could see in me was another pastor who wasn't willing to listen with an open heart. A few days later, he approached me.

"You didn't even take the time to hear me out," he said. "I believe this is what God wants me to do. I thought you were different from other pastors, but all you care about is what is going to help you and the numbers where you are right now. What if God is opening this door for us to reach a new community? How will we know if we don't walk through it?"

Immediately, I knew that he was right. I really was just being selfish about the numbers at my own church. I wasn't thinking about how the opportunity could benefit Rich or any of his young athletes.

CONFLICT AND RELATIONSHIP

Believe it or not, God used this moment to draw Rich and me closer together. Rich was honest about his disappointment and didn't try to hurt me back. When we handle conflict correctly, everyone learns from his or her mistakes and grows into greater maturity. The church that handles conflict well will continue to grow stronger and will become a bright light in the community.

I believe that the main reason most people today don't have deep relationships is that conflict sends us running. We hold on to our bruises and bring them with us to the next Christian family instead of taking our existing relationships to the next level. Avoiding conflict may seem easy initially, but the result will be a heart polluted with unhealed wounds and crippling bitterness.

If we want to have strong and lasting relationships in our churches, families, and communities, we need to learn to talk with others respectfully and gently when they hurt us. If we are willing to be honest and allow others to speak from their hearts in return, we will find peace and acceptance that we didn't know was possible here on earth.

Using the Matthew 18 principle to sow honesty and forgiveness will result in a harvest of meaningful relationships that's well worth the effort. You will show others that you can overcome hurt and continue growing in a relationship. Your family, your friends, and your health will thank you for the rest of your life.

About the Author

Chip Nightingale is a pastor, international conference and Bible teacher, entrepreneur, and leadership coach. He loves coaching sports and encouraging leaders through coaching in business and in the church. He currently serves as the Director of Advancement at Word of Life Fellowship. Chip lives in Hudson, Florida, with his wife, Audrey, and they have four amazing children.

About Renown Publishing

Renown Publishing was founded with one mission in mind: to make your great idea famous.

At Renown Publishing, we don't just publish. We work hard to pair strategy with innovative marketing techniques so that your book launch is the start of something bigger.

Learn more at RenownPublishing.com.

Notes

1. Sonksen, Chris. "When Is It OK to Quit Church? Here Are Five Reasons to Leave." *Fox News.* July 14, 2018. https://www.foxnews.com/opinion/when-is-it-ok-to-quit-church-here-are-five-reasons-to-leave.

2. Sonksen, "When Is It OK to Quit Church?"

3. Mayo Clinic. "Forgiveness: Letting Go of Grudges and Bitterness." https://www.mayoclinic.org/healthy-lifestyle/adult-health/in-depth/forgiveness/art-20047692.

4. *Thayer's Greek Lexicon,* "Strong's G266 – *hamartia.*" In Blue Letter Bible.

https://www. blueletterbible.org/lexicon/g266/kjv/tr/0-1/.

5. Blue Letter Bible, "Strong's H2398 – *ḥāṭā'.*" https://www. blueletterbible.org/lexicon/h2398/kjv/wlc/0-1/.

6. Wiersbe, Warren W. *The Bible Exposition Commentary.* Vol. 1. Victor Books, 1996, p. 66.

7. Wiersbe, *The Bible Exposition Commentary*, p. 67.

8. Kind Snacks. "Our Journey Inspiring Kindness." https://www. kindsnacks.com/our-mission-inspiring-kindness.html.

9. Ellen Digital Ventures. "The Winter Box Is Here." Be Kind By Ellen. 2021. https://www.bekindbyellen.com/?gclid=Cj0KCQ jwpreJBhDvARIs-AF1_BU2ZRKYDugx9BU75qWeMBdA45lC J8WfI-9GWt5cbhGV9TtVL5UacaiAaArB2EALw_wcB.

10. Evans, Tony. "Message 3: Encountering God's Promises." https://go.tonyevans.org/hubfs/docs/Divine%20Encounters%20 Teaching%20Outline%203.pdf.

Made in the USA
Middletown, DE
16 September 2022